Bilingual Picture Dictionaries

My First Book of
Polish
Words

by Katy R. Kudela

Translator: Translations.com

apple
jabłko
(YAHP-koh)

a Capstone company — publishers for children

Contents

How to use this dictionary

This book is full of useful words in both Polish and English. The English word appears first, followed by the Polish word. Look below each Polish word for help to sound it out. Try reading the words aloud.

Topic heading in English

Topic heading in Polish

Word in English
Word in Polish
(pronunciation)

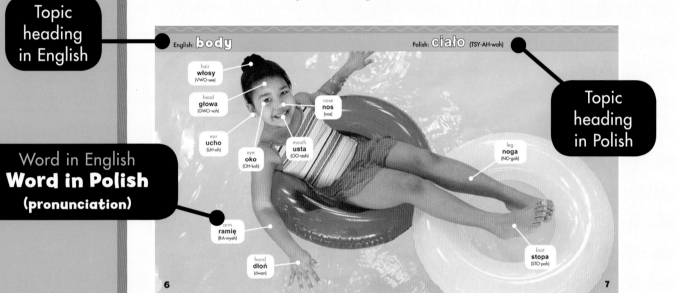

English: **body**

Polish: **ciało** (TSY-AH-woh)

hair
włosy
(VWO-see)

head
głowa
(GWO-wah)

nose
nos
(nos)

ear
ucho
(UH-oh)

mouth
usta
(OO-stah)

eye
oko
(OH-koh)

leg
noga
(NO-gah)

arm
ramię
(RA-myeh)

hand
dłoń
(dwan)

foot
stopa
(STO-pah)

6

7

Notes about the Polish language

The Polish language uses the same alphabet as English, but there are a few letters with accent marks. These letters include: ą, ć, ę, ł, ń, ó, ś, ź and ż. To read the Polish letters, look at the pronunciation. The pronunciations can be read like English.

In many pronunciations, the letter "h" is added after a vowel. The "h" is to show a reader that the vowel can be read like English, such as "ah" for "a" and "oh" for "o."

In Polish, some letters are pronounced differently depending upon where they are used. Listed below are examples of some of these sounds.

ch = same as the letter "h"

cz = hard "ch" sound, as in "church," "cheese," or "chicken"

dz = as in "reD Zone"

dz followed by an "i" = "j" as in "jeep"

rz = hard "sh" sound

sz = "sh" sound, as in "shirt" or "shoes"

szcz = combination of both as the "shch" as in "freSH CHeese"

uncle
wujek
(VOO-yehk)

mother
mama
(MAH-mah)

cousin
kuzyn
(KOO-zihn)

aunt
ciotka
(TSY-OHT-kah)

baby
niemowlę
(nye-MOH-vleh)

4

grandmother
babcia
(BAB-tsy-ah)

father
tata
(TAH-tah)

grandfather
dziadek
(DJIAH-deck)

brother
brat
(braht)

sister
siostra
(SYOH-strah)

5

hair
włosy
(VWOH-sih)

head
głowa
(GWOH-vah)

ear
ucho
(OO-hoh)

eye
oko
(OH-koh)

nose
nos
(NOHS)

mouth
usta
(OO-stah)

arm
ramię
(RAH-myeh)

hand
dłoń
(dwon)

leg
noga
(NOH-gah)

foot
stopa
(STOH-pah)

coat
kurtka
(KOOR-tkah)

pyjamas
piżama
(pee-JA-mah)

shorts
szorty
(SHOR-tee)

boot
kalosz
(KAH-losh)

ROAR!
I'm the loudest in the jungle

8

shoe
but
(boot)

hat
czapka
(CHAP-kah)

trousers
spodnie
(SPOH-dnyeh)

sock
skarpeta
(skar-PEH-tah)

dress
sukienka
(soo-KYEN-kah)

shirt
koszula
(koh-SHOO-lah)

9

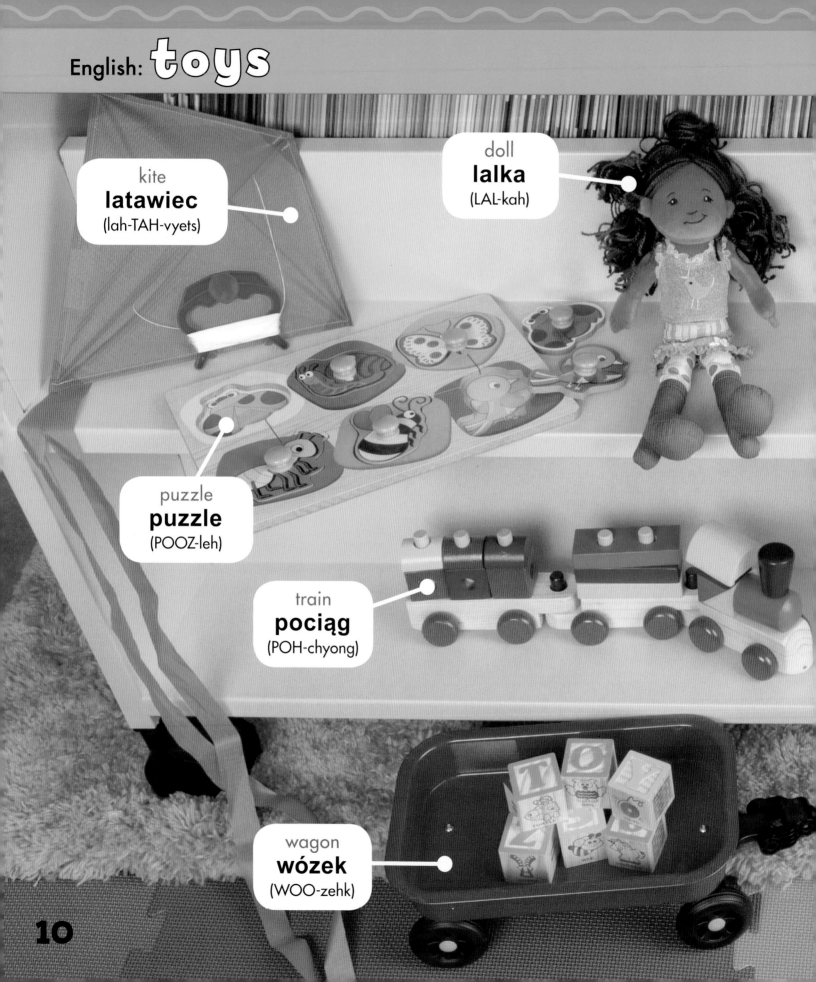

kite
latawiec
(lah-TAH-vyets)

doll
lalka
(LAL-kah)

puzzle
puzzle
(POOZ-leh)

train
pociąg
(POH-chyong)

wagon
wózek
(WOO-zehk)

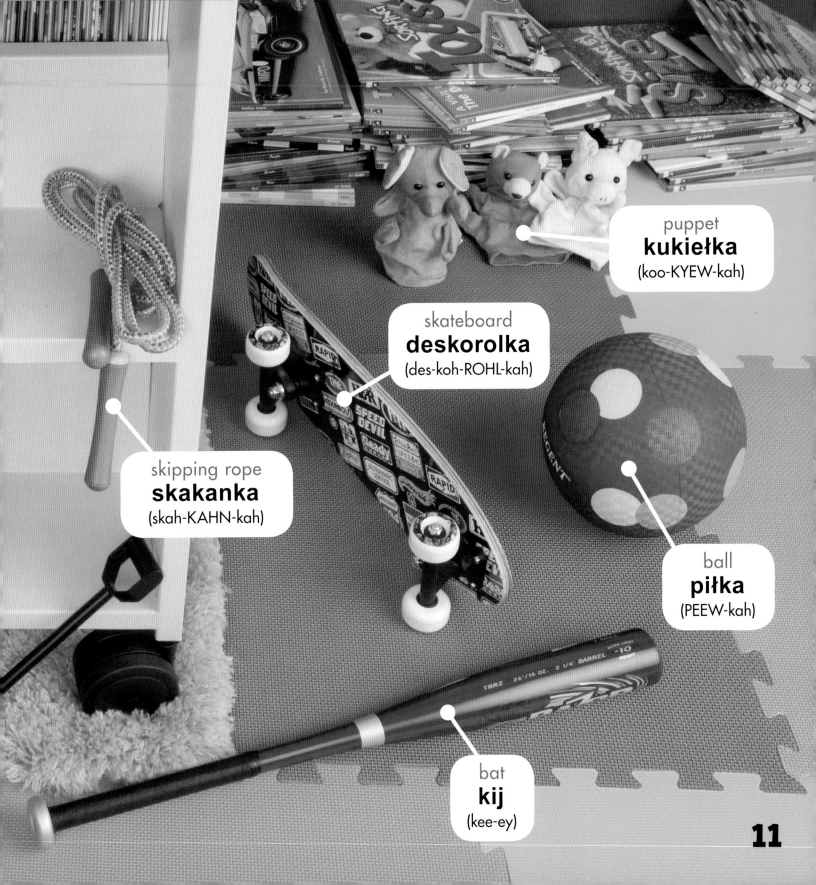

puppet
kukiełka
(koo-KYEW-kah)

skateboard
deskorolka
(des-koh-ROHL-kah)

skipping rope
skakanka
(skah-KAHN-kah)

ball
piłka
(PEEW-kah)

bat
kij
(kee-ey)

11

window
okno
(OHK-noh)

picture
obraz
(OHB-rahz)

lamp
lampa
(LAM-pah)

chest of
drawers
komoda
(koh-MOH-dah)

curtain
zasłona
(za-SWOH-nah)

blanket
koc
(kohts)

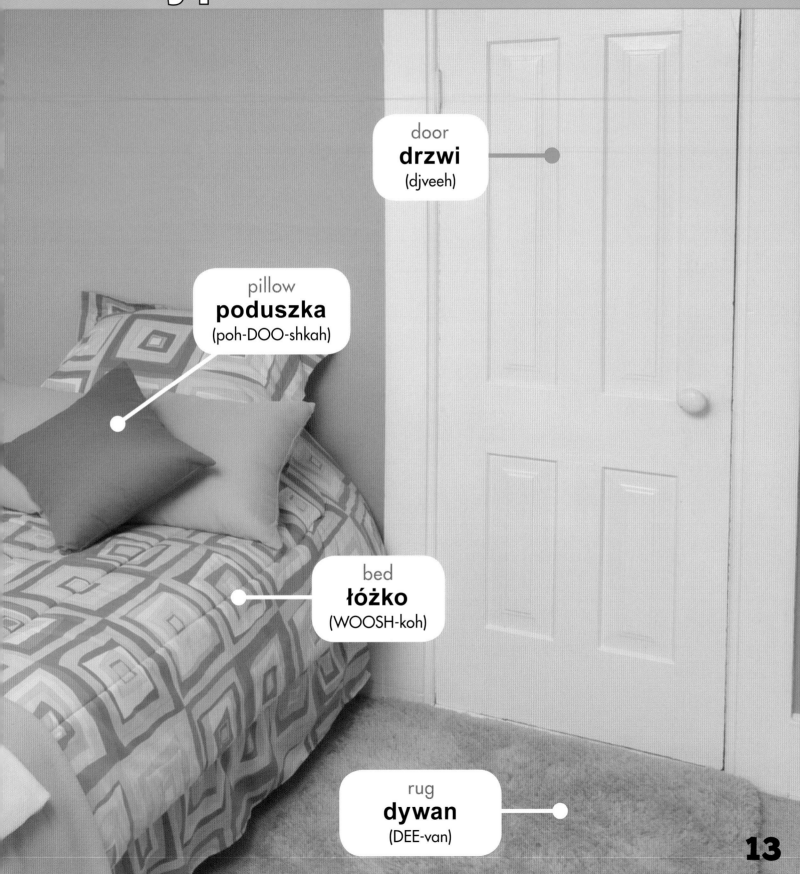

door
drzwi
(djveeh)

pillow
poduszka
(poh-DOO-shkah)

bed
łóżko
(WOOSH-koh)

rug
dywan
(DEE-van)

13

bath
wanna
(VAHN-nah)

soap
mydło
(MEED-woh)

toilet
muszla
(MOOSH-lah)

Polish: **łazienka** (wa-ZHYEN-kah)

mirror
lustro
(loo-stroh)

toothbrush
szczoteczka do zębów
(shchoh-TETSH-kah doh ZEM-boof)

toothpaste
pasta do zębów
(PAH-stah doh ZEM-boof)

comb
grzebień
(GSHEH-byenh)

sink
umywalka
(oo-mee-VAHL-kah)

towel
ręcznik
(RENCH-neek)

brush
szczotka do włosów
(SHCHOT-kah doh VWOH-soof)

pot
garnek
(GAHR-nehk)

hob
kuchenka
(koo-HEN-kah)

bowl
miska
(MEES-kah)

oven
piec
(pyets)

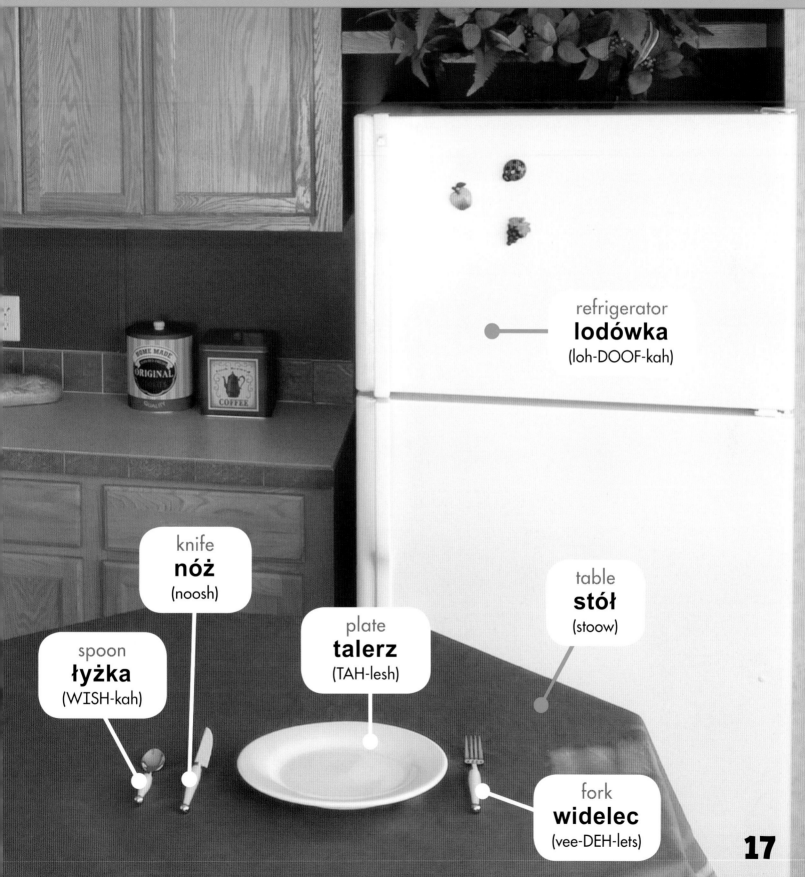

Polish: **kuchnia** (KOOH-nyah)

refrigerator
lodówka
(loh-DOOF-kah)

knife
nóż
(noosh)

table
stół
(stoow)

plate
talerz
(TAH-lesh)

spoon
łyżka
(WISH-kah)

fork
widelec
(vee-DEH-lets)

17

milk
mleko
(MLEH-koh)

carrot
marchewka
(mahr-HEF-kah)

bread
chleb
(hlep)

apple
jabłko
(YAHP-koh)

butter
masło
(MAS-woh)

18

egg
jajko
(YUY-koh)

pea
groszek
(GROH-shek)

orange
pomarańcza
(poh-mah-RAHN-chah)

sandwich
kanapka
(kah-NAHP-kah)

rice
ryż
(rish)

tractor
traktor
(TRAC-tor)

hay
siano
(SHYA-noh)

fence
płot
(PWOHT)

farmer
rolnik
(ROL-nick)

sheep
owca
(OF-tsah)

pig
świnia
(SHVEE-nyah)

Polish: **gospodarstwo** (gos-po-DAR-stvoh)

horse
koń
(kohn)

barn
stodoła
(stoh-DOH-wah)

cow
krowa
(KROH-vah)

chicken
kurczak
(KOOR-chuck)

leaf
liść
(LEE-SIH-TSIH)

butterfly
motyl
(MOH-tihl)

flower
kwiat
(KVEE-yaht)

trowel
łopata
(woh-PAH-tah)

bird
ptak
(ptahk)

worm
dżdżownica
(dj-djoh-NEEH-tsah)

Polish: **ogród** (OG-root)

plant
roślina
(roh-SHLEE-nah)

grass
trawa
(TRAH-vah)

soil
ziemia
(ZYEH-myah)

seed
ziarno
(ZYAR-noh)

23

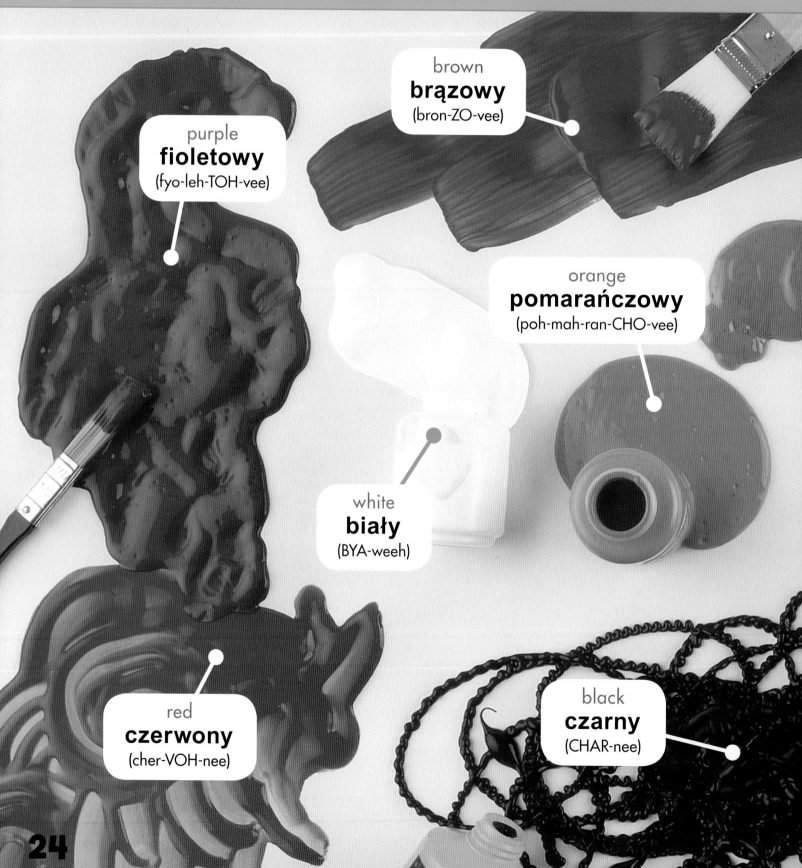

brown
brązowy
(bron-ZO-vee)

purple
fioletowy
(fyo-leh-TOH-vee)

orange
pomarańczowy
(poh-mah-ran-CHO-vee)

white
biały
(BYA-weeh)

red
czerwony
(cher-VOH-nee)

black
czarny
(CHAR-nee)

pink
różowy
(roo-ZHOH-vee)

blue
niebieski
(nye-BYE-skee)

yellow
żółty
(ZHOOW-tee)

green
zielony
(zyeh-LOH-nee)

teacher
nauczyciel
(nah-oo-CHEE-tchel)

book
książka
(KSHY-ONSH-kah)

desk
biurko
(BYOOR-koh)

pencil
ołówek
(oh-WOO-vek)

crayon
kredka
(KRET-kah)

map
mapa
(MAH-pah)

clock
zegar
(ZEH-gahr)

computer
komputer
(com-POO-ter)

chair
krzesło
(KSHE-swoh)

paper
papier
(PAH-pyer)

traffic light
światła
(SHVYA-tlah)

library
biblioteka
(bee-blyo-TEH-kah)

shop
sklep
(sklep)

bicycle
rower
(ROH-ver)

car
samochód
(sah-MOH-hood)

LIBRARY

ONE WAY

Tuesday 2:00-5:00
Thursday 2:00-6:00

28

Polish: **miasto** (MY-AS-toh)

tree
drzewo
(JEH-voh)

bus
autobus
(auw-TOH-boos)

park
park
(park)

street
ulica
(OO-LEE-tsa)

sign
znak
(znahk)

STOP

29

Numbers • Liczby (LEETCH-bee)

1. one • **jeden** (YEH-dehn)
2. two • **dwa** (dvah)
3. three • **trzy** (tshee)
4. four • **cztery** (CHTEH-ree)
5. five • **pięć** (pyentsh)

6. six • **sześć** (sheshch)
7. seven • **siedem** (SYEH-dehm)
8. eight • **osiem** (OH-syem)
9. nine • **dziewięć** (DSJEH-vyehntsh)
10. ten • **dziesięć** (DSJEH-syehntsh)

Useful phrases • Przydatne zwroty (pshee-DAT-neh ZVRO-tee)

yes • **tak** (takh)

no • **nie** (nyeh)

hello • **cześć** (tcheshch)

goodbye • **do widzenia** (doh vi-DSEN-ee-ah)

good morning • **dzień dobry** (djen DOH-bree)

goodnight • **dobranoc** (do-BRAH-nots)

please • **proszę** (PROH-sheh)

thank you • **dziękuję** (djen-KOO-yah)

excuse me • **przepraszam** (pshe-PRAH-sham)

My name is _____. • **Nazywam się** _____. (nah-ZI-vahm syeh)